HEAVEN AND MIRTH®

Daniel
Nice Kitty!

AND
OTHER BIBLE STORIES TO TICKLE YOUR SOUL

by Mike Thaler

Illustrated by Dennis Adler

*Equiping Kids
for Life*

A Faith Parenting Guide can be found on page 32.

Dedicated to
Allan and Eunice Hansen,
God's love by example.
Mike

Faith Kids™ is an imprint of
Cook Communications, Colorado Springs, Colorado 80918
Cook Communications, Paris, Ontario
Kingsway Communications, Eastbourne, England

Published in association with the literary agency of Alive Communications, Inc.,
1465 Kelly Johnson Blvd., Suite 320, Colorado Springs CO 80920.

Edited by Jeannie Harmon
Design by Clyde Van Cleve

First hardcover printing, 2000
Printed in the Singapore
04 03 02 01 00   5 4 3 2 1

Library of Congress Cataloging-in-Publication Data
Thaler, Mike, 1936-
        Daniel, nice kitty! and other Bible stories to tickle your soul/by Mike
Thaler; illustrated by Dennis Adler.
            p. cm. -- (Heaven and Mirth)
        Summary: five stories written in a humorous vein, based on incidents
taken from the Old Testament and focusing on the importance of having faith.
        ISBN 0-7814-3432-7
        1. Bible stories, English--O.T. 2. Bible. O.T.--Juvenile humor. [I. Bible
stories--O.T.] I. Adler, Dennis (Dennis H.), 1942- ill.
II. Title.
BS551.2.T444 2000
221.9'505--dc21
                                                    00-025327

Letter from the Author

Taking this opportunity, I would like to share with you how this book came about. Born sixty-two years ago, I have been a secular children's book author most of my life. I was also content to have a fast-food relationship with God from the drive-by window. At the age of sixty, I came into the banquet by inviting Jesus Christ into my heart. Since then my life has been a glorious feast. These stories are part of that celebration.

One night I sat and watched a sincere grandfather trying to read Bible stories to his squirming grandchildren. I asked him, "Aren't there any humorous retellings of Bible stories that are vivid and alive for kids?" He rolled his eyes and said, "This is it." The kids rolled their eyes, too.

This made me sad, for the Bible is the most exciting, valuable, and alive book I know—as is its Author. So I went into my room, with this in mind, and wrote "Noah's Rainbow."

Since then God has anointed me with sixty stories that fire my imagination and light up my heart. They are stories which, I hope, are filled with the joy, love, and spirit of the Lord.

Mike Thaler
West Linn 1998

Nuggets from Goldie the miner prophet:
"It's Never Too Late to Eat Right."

Author's Note

I have conscientiously tried to follow each story in word and spirit as found in the Bible. But in some cases, for the sake of storytelling, I have taken minor liberties and added small details. I pray for your understanding in these instances.

3

Moses

Good Help Is Hard to Find

LONG BEFORE THERE WERE CELL PHONES, God used a burning bush to call people. When the Israelites were slaves in Egypt, God called a man named Moses and told him to tell the *Unfair-oh* to let God's people go.

"Why me, Lord?" asked Moses. "When I was a kid, I was a basket case."

"You're My guy," said God, and He gave Moses three magic tricks to do.

The first was throwing down his staff which turned into a wriggling snake. The second was a simple blight of hand trick involving a major disease. And the third was pulling two scarves out of Pharaoh's ears.

With his brother Aaron, Moses went to Pharaoh
and did God's tricks. Pharaoh was not impressed.
In fact, he doubled the Israelites' workload.

"We were better off before you butted in," everyone complained
"If you see Pharaoh again, he'll probably take away
our coffee break and cancel our bowling league."

"Be cool," said Moses. "The Lord our God
is watching over you,
and will never let you lose
your health plan."

Next, God told Moses
to tell Pharaoh he was going to send
horrible plagues upon Egypt,
and God did.

The first was blood.
Pharaoh was about to take his morning dip
in the Nile, and Moses struck the water with his staff.
It turned into a river of blood.

"Big deal," said Pharaoh's magicians,
and they tapped Pharaoh's *Perrier,*
and it turned into blood too.

"Hey," said Pharaoh, "this is great.
Call the Red Cross."

The second was frogs.
There were frogs everywhere,
with a *ribbit ribbit* here
and a *ribbit ribbit* there.
French restaurants did great.
Everyone else had open toad
shoes, and even though
Pharaoh was hopping mad,
he still said, "No."

"What next?" asked Moses.

"Gnats," said God.

"Nix," said Pharaoh.

"Next," said Moses.

"I'll send flies," said God.
Instantly, the land filled with flies.
There were flies in left field,
flies in right field,
and pop flies in center.
Pharaoh called out his S.W.A.T. team,
and the flies didn't help the Israelites flee.

Then Moses raised his staff
and all the Egyptian cows
died from a staff infection.

"Where's the beef?"
asked Pharaoh at dinner.
  "Get the Hamburger Helper."

Next God sent boils.
Everyone had boils.
It was a dermatologist's dream.

Pharaoh blustered,
  "You haven't boiled me over yet."

  "He's hardboiled," said Moses.

"Let's try hail," thundered God.

"Cool it," said Pharaoh,
"We got umbrellas."

"Let's try locusts,"
said God.

Munch, munch, munch.
Suddenly, there were
bunches of munches
having Egypt for lunches.
Pharaoh was bugged
but he wouldn't bite.

"He's tough," said Moses.

"I'm tougher," said God.
"It's time to get serious."

God closed His eyes and darkness descended upon Egypt.

"It's not so bad," said Pharaoh. "We got candles."

"OK," said God,
"This one's My top-of-the-line plague.
Every firstborn kid in Egypt
will turn into a teenager."

A great moan went through the land
and Pharaoh said, "Go, go, go."

Quickly, all the Israelites packed their stuff
and hit the road.

But after they had gone
   and Pharaoh had to make his own bagels,
      straighten his kid's teeth,
       and figure out his income tax,
        he wanted them back.
         He jumped into his chariot,
            and with his army, chased the Israelites
               to the edge of the Red Sea.

When the Israelites saw
   the approaching soldiers,
      they complained bitterly.
      "Things weren't so bad
         back in Egypt.
      We were only whipped
         every other day,
            now we'll be shot with arrows,
            or worse, drowned."

"Have faith, the Lord your God
did not bring you here to die."

Then Moses raised up his staff
and the Red Sea parted before them.

"We knew it all the time," said the Israelites,
and they skipped across safely.

When the Egyptians followed,
the sea closed around them and they drowned
to the last man and the last horse.
This really impressed the Israelites.

"God is a great lifeguard!"
And they vowed in the future
to listen to Him
whenever they were in hot water.

THE END

Nuggets from Goldie the miner prophet:

"With God, you either play ball or plague all!"

For the real story, read Exodus 1–15.

Absalom
Rebel without a Hair Net

ABSALOM WAS A DISOBEDIENT SON.
He wouldn't straighten up his room,
he let his hair grow long, and he killed his brother.
His father King David, always forgave him
and made excuses for him.

"He's just hyperactive and he'd be so good looking,
if only he would get a haircut."

Absalom was *so* handsome
that everyone else forgave him too.

He would run around town
in his sport chariot
with his long hair
flowing in the breeze,
and everyone
would admire him.
Nobody seemed to mind
that he went through
red lights, ran over chickens,
and drove on the sidewalk.

"He's just spirited," they would say.

But Absalom was mean-spirited.
And all the while, he was planning
to kill his father and become king.

When David's friends told him,
the king said, "He's just an overachiever."

Even when Absalom gathered an army
to march on the palace,
David lamented, "He's always been an ambitious lad."

However, this time David *had* to discipline him.

The king gathered his own army.
He commanded them, "Don't hurt Absalom,
just capture him, and I'll ground him for a week."

They met in battle
and Absalom's army was defeated.
While he was trying to escape,
his long hair got stuck
in the branches of a tree,
and Joab, one of David's generals
who knew Absalom was a real punk,
punctured him with three spears.
It was a *real* bad hair day.

When David heard
that his son was dead,
he cried, "This has been
a hair-raising
experience."

THE END

Nuggets from Goldie the miner prophet:
"It's better to have bad hair than a bad heir."

For the real story, read 2 Samuel 14–18.

Naaman

Can a Leper Change His Spots?

NAAMAN WAS A SOLDIER,
but he couldn't pass his physical.
He had *leprosy*.
Luckily, he had recently captured
a maid from Israel.
Good help was easy to find
in those days.
She did windows, and she knew
of a prophet in Israel
who had healed warts.
So Naaman's boss, the King of Aram,
told him to check it out.
He even wrote a note to his troops.

Naaman is missing the battle today
because he has leprosy and is going to get cured.

Naaman took ten talents of silver and six thousand shekels of gold. (They didn't have health plans in those days.) Then he went to the King of Israel.

The king read the note and overreacted a little. He jumped up and down and tore his clothes.

"I can't cure you. Who do you think I am? God? I'm just an ear, nose, and throat king!"

When Elisha the prophet heard that the monarch had torn his clothes, he sent him a needle, thread, and a message:
"Cool it! Just send the guy to me."

Naaman took his horses and his chariots, made a two o'clock anointment, and went to see Elisha. But Elisha sent out his nurse.

"Fill out these forms," he said, handing Naaman a clipboard stacked with forms, "and fill this cup."

Naaman spent three days filling out the forms and filling up the cup.★

★It was a big cup.

At the end of the three days,
the nurse came back
and told him to have a seat.
A week later, after Naaman had
read every magazine
in the prophet's waiting room,
sixty issues of *Raising Hamsters
for Fun and Prophets,*
the nurse came back
and told him to go wash
in the River Jordan
seven times.
Naaman became furious.

"This is what I traveled a hundred miles for?
I could have been treated like this at home."

But a wise servant came to him and said:

"Listen, Boss, if the prophet himself had talked fancy,
how much better off would you be?
Go wash and see what happens."

So Naaman followed the prescription
and dipped in the Jordan seven times.
And lo and behold, he was cured!
His clothes shrunk, but he was cured of leprosy.
His flesh was restored and became clean

like that of a young boy. That means he had pimples,
but pimples are better than leprosy any day.
So Naaman went back to the prophet.

"You did it! You have the one and only true God.
How much do I owe you?"

"It's on the house," said Elisha. "God is free."

"I will honor your God forever and never bow down
before any other gods, unless of course, my boss is leaning on me."

"Get outta here," said Elisha.

Naaman took off.
But Elisha's nurse,
Gehazi, thought:
*Hey, why pass up
all this booty?*
So he took off
after Naaman.

When Naaman saw Gehazi coming
he asked, "Is everything OK?
"Well," said Gehazi, "I checked,
and your health plan doesn't cover river dipping
so I'm afraid it'll have to be cash after all."

"Sure," said Naaman. "Take what you like."

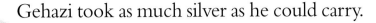

Gehazi took as much silver as he could carry.

When he got back to the office, Elisha asked him,
    "Where have you been?"

"Nowhere."

"Why are your pockets
full of silver?"

"Tips!"

"Hey, do you think you can fool
a major prophet? I see all and know all.
You've taxed my patients for the last time."

"Someday, everybody will," cried Gehazi.

"Don't nurse it, you just won Naaman's leprosy
for yourself and all your descendants forever.
And by the way, you're fired."

THE END

Nuggets from Goldie the miner prophet:
"With the help of God, even a leper can change his spots."

For the real story, read 2 Kings 5.

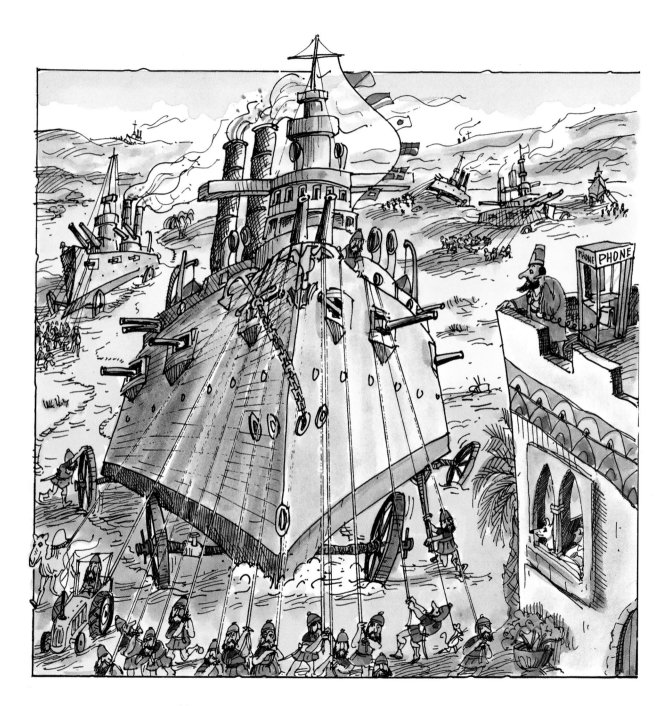

Hezekiah

My God Can Beat Up Your God

HEZEKIAH WAS A GOOD KING because he was a true servant of God. But when he heard the whole Assyrian army was marching to attack Jerusalem, he got frightened. He called out the militia, the veterans of foreign wars, and the navy, which was difficult, since they were in the middle of the desert.

He started turning off all the drinking fountains outside the city, building up the walls with Legos, and handing out Swiss Army knives.

He also mobilized the Brownies,
who started baking cookies for the siege.

When *Snackribs*, King of Assyria, arrived,
he started sending Hezekiah nasty notes.

Hezekiah, your God is a wimp.
He can't protect you.
He can't save you.
He's a party pooper.

Hezekiah sat on the wall.
Hezekiah had a great fall.
All the king's horses and all the king's men
Couldn't put Hezekiah together again.

Yo, Hezekiah, nobody's God
has been able to stop me and my dad.
We've creamed kingdoms
all over this desert.
We're a lean mean fighting machine.
So tremble in your sandals.

The Assyrian army also ran around the city
shouting, "Our god can lick your God.
Na-Na-Na-Na-Na!"

Hezekiah got really scared. He went to the Prophet Isaiah
and told him what *Snackribs* had said.
Isaiah told God, and God got really miffed.

"He called me a what?" shouted God. **"A wimp, huh!"** thundered God. **"Well, don't worry guys, I'll make short work of *Snackribs* and from this day on he'll be known as *Shortribs*."**

So that night, God sent his meanest angel of death to visit the Assyrian army. And in the morning not one soldier from private to general was left alive. However, God did spare *Shortribs,* and from that day on he was known as *Spareribs.*

"Well," cried *Spareribs,* "You don't fight fair down here. I'm going home where men are men, and have a sense of chivalry." Unfortunately, when he got home his two sons stabbed him in the back with large swords.

His last words were, "Ouch, ouch!"

And so God saved Hezekiah and Jerusalem, and when the word got around, *everybody* took their hats off to God from then on.

THE END

Nuggets from Goldie the miner prophet:
"God says, 'Leave the driving to Me!'"

For the real story, read 2 Kings 18–19.

Daniel
Nice Kitty!

Daniel was allergic to cats. Luckily, they were allergic to him too.

When King Darius the Mede took over the Babylonian Empire, he appointed 120 *ratraps*★ to run the kingdom. Over them, he appointed three big cheeses.

Now, Daniel was such an overacheeser
that Darius finally made him
the biggest cheese in the kingdom.
The 120 *ratraps* did not like this,
and they tried to catch Daniel doing something wrong.
But it was not a snap, for Daniel was neither
negligent nor dishonest.

★Fat cat bureaucrats really called *satraps*.

Joining together, they formed the *Diligent Dan Unfan Club*, and came up with a plan to bring Dan down.

They went directly to King Darius and told him to issue a royal decree that no one in his kingdom should pray to anyone else but him for the next 30 days.
It was sort of an Honor Darius Month. Darius, like most kings, was not humble, so he signed it.

When Daniel heard about the decree, he went home and prayed. But, of course, he prayed to God Almighty.
All the ratraps saw him and ran back to the king.

"O, King," they snitched, "We saw Daniel praying to a God other than you. What are you going to do about it?"

King Darius valued Daniel and didn't want him turned into a *Fancy Feast*, which was the penalty for inappropriate praying.

He called Daniel to him.
"Dan, I bet you were really
praying to me, right?"

"No," said Daniel. "I wasn't."

"Dan, I bet just this month
you'd pray to me a little."

"Sorry, I can't," said Daniel.

"See!" cried all the ratraps.
"What are ya gonna to do
about it, *huh?!*"

There was no escape clause,
so Darius had to throw Daniel
to the lions and seal the den.
But he felt really bad
and couldn't sleep all night.
Early the next morning, he ran back.

"Daniel! Daniel!" he shouted.
"Is there anything left of you?"

"Lots!" shouted Daniel.

"Thank God your Lord is a Den Father."

"He sure is. Not one feline made a beeline for me,

but could you get me outta here?
The kitty litter hasn't been changed
in weeks."

So Daniel was brought outta the den
without a scratch on 'im,
and all his accusers were thrown in.

Now, the cats hadn't eaten all night,
and they were really hungry.
So they totally gobbled up
the *Diligent Dan Unfan Club*.

Then, Darius,
who was very impressed,
signed a new decree for all his kingdom:

Now hear this:
From now on
Daniel's God is the God for us!
He's the one and only, not a phony!
He's first rate, really great
He gives me the shivers
'cause he delivers.
Ah-h-hmen

Signed,
Darius the Humble

And Daniel did really well from then on,
'cause everyone knew he was a cool cat
with a real tiger in his tank.

THE END

Nuggets from Goldie the miner prophet:
"When you're a loyal scout, God is a faithful Den Father."

For the real story, read Daniel 6.

HEAVEN AND MIRTH®

Daniel
Nice Kitty!

Age: 6 and up

Life Issue: Learning to have faith in God, no matter
what the circumstances.

Spiritual Building Block: Faith

Learning Styles

Help your child learn about faith in the following ways:

Sight: View a story video about Moses, Daniel in the Lion's den, Queen Esther, Elijah and the prophets of Baal, or Jonah. How did their faith in God help them when the going got tough? How can your faith in God help you when difficult circumstances come?

Sound: As you and your child sit with extended family member, talk about times when God has met a special need or helped you out of a difficult situation. Ask others to contribute their own stories. Sharing stories like these builds faith in the hearts of young listeners.

Touch: Take two puzzles the difficulty level appropriate to your child's age. Place the pieces of one puzzle on the end of a table with the box in plain view. A picture of the completed puzzle should be on the cover. Place the pieces of the other puzzle at the opposite end of the table with no box in view. Which puzzle is easier to assemble? Why? The Bible gives us many examples of how God cares for people. When we read the Bible, we get a picture of what His love and care is like. As we face difficult situations, we can remember these examples and believe that God will take care of us just as He has done many times in the past.

Adapted from *Wisdom Life Skills* by Jim Weidmann and Kurt Bruner,
published by Chariot Victor Publishing, page 101.